ALSO AVAILABLE IN THIS SERIES:
BELIEVE: The Words and Inspiration of Desmond Tutu
PEACE: The Words and Inspiration of Mahatma Gandhi
DREAM: The Words and Inspiration of Martin Luther King, Jr.

Produced and originated by PQ Blackwell Limited
116 Symonds Street, Auckland, New Zealand
www.pqblackwell.com

Distributed exclusively in the United States, Canada, and the Philippines by Blue
Mountain Arts, Inc.

Designed by Cameron Gibb, Annatjie Matthee, and Carolyn Lewis.

Printed by Midas Printing International Ltd., China.

Library of Congress Control Number: 2006909705
ISBN: 978-1-59842-243-6

Acknowledgments appear on page 94.

First Printing: 2007

Blue Mountain Arts, Inc.

P.O. Box 4549, Boulder, Colorado 80306

THE WORDS AND INSPIRATION OF

MOTHER TERESA

LOVE

INTRODUCTION BY
ARCHBISHOP DESMOND TUTU

Blue Mountain Press ®

Boulder, Colorado

"If I diminish you, I diminish myself."

In my culture and tradition the highest praise that can be given to someone is, "*Yu, u nobuntu*," an acknowledgment that he or she has this wonderful quality: *ubuntu*. It is a reference to their actions toward their fellow human beings, it has to do with how they regard people and how they see themselves within their intimate relationships, their familial relationships, and within the broader community. *Ubuntu* addresses a central tenet of African philosophy: the essence of what it is to be human.

The definition of this concept has two parts. The first is that the person is friendly, hospitable, generous, gentle, caring, and compassionate. In other words, someone who will use their strengths on behalf of others — the weak and the poor and the ill — and not take advantage of anyone. This person treats others as he or she would be treated. And because of this they express the second part of the concept, which concerns openness, large-heartedness. They share their worth. In doing so my humanity is recognized and becomes inextricably bound to theirs.

People with *ubuntu* are approachable and welcoming; their attitude is kindly and well-disposed; they are not threatened by the goodness in others because their own esteem and self-worth is generated by knowing they belong to a greater whole. To recast the Cartesian proposition "I think, therefore I am," *ubuntu* would phrase it, "I am human because I belong." Put another way, "a person is a person through other people," a concept perfectly captured by the phrase "me we." No one comes into the world fully formed. We would not know how to think or walk or speak or behave unless we learned it from our fellow human beings. We need other human beings in order to be human. The solitary, isolated human being is a contradiction in terms.

Because we need one another, our natural tendency is to be cooperative and helpful. If this were not true we would have died out as a species long ago, consumed by our violence and hate. But we haven't. We have kept on despite the evil and the wars that have brought so much suffering and misery down the centuries. We have kept on because we strive for harmony and community, a community not only of the living but also one that honors our forebears. This link to the past gives us a sense of continuity, a sense that we have created and create societies that are meant to be for the greater good and try to overcome anything that subverts our purpose. Our wars end; we seek to heal.

But anger, resentment, a lust for revenge, greed, even the aggressive competitiveness that rules so much of our contemporary world, corrodes and jeopardizes our harmony. *Ubuntu* points out that those who seek to destroy and dehumanize are also victims — victims, usually, of a pervading ethos, be it a political ideology, an economic system, or a distorted religious conviction. Consequently, they are as much dehumanized as those on whom they trample.

Never was this more obvious than during the apartheid years in South Africa. All humanity is interlinked. Thus, the humanity of the perpetrators of apartheid was inexorably bound to that of their victims. When they dehumanized another by inflicting suffering and harm, they dehumanized themselves. In fact I said at the time that the oppressor was dehumanized as much as, if not more than, those oppressed. How else could you interpret the words of the minister of police, Jimmy Kruger, on hearing of the death of Black Consciousness leader, Steve Biko, in prison. Of his tortured and painful killing, Kruger said, it "leaves me cold." You have to ask what has happened to the humanity — the *ubuntu* — of someone who could speak so callously about the suffering and death of a fellow human being.

It was equally clear that recovering from this situation would require a magnanimousness on the part of the victims if there was to be a future. The end of apartheid, I knew, would put *ubuntu* to the test. Yet I never doubted its power of reconciliation. In fact I often recalled the words of a man called Malusi Mpumlwana, an associate of Biko's, who, even while he was being tortured by the security police, looked at his torturers and realized that these were human beings too and that they needed him "to help them recover the humanity they [were] losing."

This is the essence of *ubuntu*, or "me we," and in this are reflected vividly the life and actions of Mother Teresa. Her entire being was focused on bringing some dignity and compassion into the lives of the destitute and the afflicted. In a world that is hard and cynical, she showed that great things can be achieved wherever there is great love, not only among the desperate of Calcutta but throughout the world.

The *ubuntu* of Mother Teresa showed that the only way we can ever be human is together. The only way we can be free is together.

The Most Reverend Desmond M. Tutu, OMSG DD FKC
Anglican Archbishop Emeritus of Cape Town

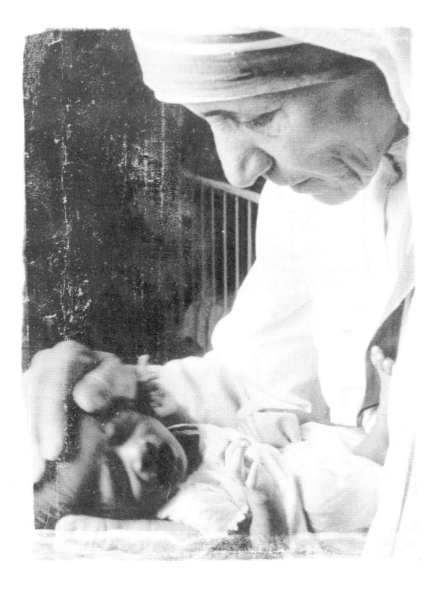

Mother Teresa

Mother Teresa of Calcutta
1910 – 1997

The nun had boarded the train in Calcutta and sat now among the pack of passengers staring out the windows at the Himalayas, vast and grand and snow-capped. She was on her way to a retreat at Darjeeling. That morning she had left the Loreto convent, a peaceful sanctuary of lush gardens and trees where she taught catechism and geography at a small exclusive school, St. Mary's. Her pupils were mostly from well-off middle-class families, but also there were included a number of orphans. The nun had entered the convent as a novitiate seventeen years previously, taken her vows, and over the years, quietly gone about her teaching, eventually becoming the school's principal.

The life of Calcutta beyond the convent was not unknown to the nun. While helping with the girls who were members of the Sodality of the Blessed Virgin Mary, she listened to their stories of visiting patients at the Nilratan Sarkar hospital, hearing about the bitter poverty of people living in the slums of the city's Motijhil district. She knew that on the other side of the convent's walls people died in misery, alone among the squalor and the dirt.

She knew too that it was a particularly desperate time in the city's history. Partition, the violent political sundering that created Pakistan, had dire consequences in Calcutta. Hostilities between Hindus and Muslims left hundreds dead in the streets, hundreds more badly wounded. The previous month, August 1946, the fighting had rendered the city a zone of horror: water was scarce or polluted, food was in short supply, and people lay dying on the streets from wounds and disease. Elsewhere the hungry and destitute picked through the refuse that had piled up, searching for anything edible. The nun had gone into these streets when food supplies failed to reach her school and had seen the city's suffering and distress. The experience had been deeply telling. Back in the convent she wondered about her life; increasingly she felt drawn to those who were outcasts, whether they had been brought to this sorry state by poverty or by illness. She saw them as the unloved, the abandoned. These thoughts troubled her as the train rattled across the Indian landscape.

Amidst this preoccupation she began to realize that she was being called to another form of work and service. She felt this as "an inner command to renounce Loreto, where I was happy, to go to serve the poor in the streets.[1] In that train I heard the call to give up all and follow him into the slums to serve him among the poorest of the poor."[2] Eventually the train arrived at Darjeeling and the nun, subdued but also inwardly exalting, began her retreat. The call continued. "The message was quite clear. It was an order. I was to leave the convent. I felt God wanted something more from me. He wanted me to be poor and to love him in the distressing disguise of the poorest of the poor."[3]

For the nun who would become the internationally renowned Mother Teresa of Calcutta, the call to serve the poor was as much an indication of her humanity as of her love of God. Where others might see two complex but related passions, the sister at the Darjeeling Hill station saw one. She could not differentiate her love of an individual from her love of God: "Every person is Christ for me, and since there is only one Jesus, that person is only one person in the world for me at that moment."[4] On two sheets of paper she wrote down what has come to be known as the "Inspiration," and when her retreat ended she took this back to her spiritual director. In short she was asking to leave the life of the cloister so that she could work on the streets among the indigent. But such requests were not simple; there were formalities to be observed. Her vows bound her to the orders of the Catholic Church, and to be released she needed permission from her convent, the church in India, and ultimately from the Vatican. This process took two years.

During that time Sister Teresa, described by those who knew her as unexceptional, a very ordinary person, went about her life and work as she had done before. Not once did she waver in her intentions or grow impatient, but waited resolutely until the release came, always convinced that what she wanted would be granted. And it was. On August 17, 1948, this small woman in her late thirties swapped the habit of a Loreto nun for a cheap white sari edged in blue. A cross was pinned to her left shoulder; on her feet were open leather sandals. She was nervous, well aware of the enormity of the moment as she closed the gate of the convent behind her. "To leave Loreto was my greatest sacrifice, the most difficult thing I have ever done. It was much more difficult than to leave my family and country to enter religious life. Loreto, my spiritual training, my work meant everything to me."[5]

Although she was leaving Loreto and was now an unenclosed nun, she believed her initial calling remained intact; she was simply going to practice what she believed. Hers was a calling — a vocation — within a calling. And it was in the vocation that the true humanity of the determined nun in the white sari hurrying through the streets of Calcutta to the train station was to be found. Sister Teresa was nothing if not pragmatic: if her future life was to be administering and tending to the sick, then she needed some form of medical training. She took a train to the town of Patna, where a group of nuns known as the Medical Missionary Sisters provided on-the-job medical training and dispensing. They had permission to practice surgery and midwifery in their hospitals, and the sister from Calcutta learned and experienced as much as she could in the short four months she spent there before returning to Calcutta. There were some at Patna who wondered if four months were sufficient induction, but the little nun was adamant: for what she had in mind she had learned enough. She hurried back to Calcutta to begin what she called her "real work."

Mother Teresa, known simply as Mother in her later decades in India, was born Agnes Gonxha Bojaxhiu on August 26, 1910 in Skopje, a small town then the capital of the Ottoman province of Kosovo. Although she was born to Albanian parents, in subsequent years her nationality was often given as Yugoslavian because politics had rearranged the Balkan landscape and incorporated the town into that troubled amalgamated state. Today the town is the capital of Macedonia.

However, to think of Mother Teresa in Eastern European terms is to miss the point of her international status: most of her life was spent in India, and when she traveled abroad it was on a diplomatic Indian passport. As she spread her work across the globe, so she became increasingly from "everywhere" rather than of any narrow nationalistic definition. This more suited her intentions of being a faceless servant of humankind than an individual known for her charity and good deeds. It also emphasized her reluctance to talk about herself or her early years in biographical terms. She would dismiss her childhood as being happy and unexceptional and try to steer the enquirer back to the terrain she wanted to publicize: the world of the mendicants and the afflicted.

She was loath to give herself a biography because that would create an individual whereas what Mother Teresa wanted was to become part of humanity, to be seen and understood in terms of human impoverishment and suffering. By negating herself nothing could happen to her; her life would have to be recorded according to her "real work" because the persona "Mother Teresa" would comprise nothing else. It was not by accident that the phrase "Yet not I, but Christ liveth in me" was one of her favorite rejoinders to any queries about the individual called Mother Teresa.

This said, her father, Nikola (Kole) Bojaxhiu, was a prosperous merchant. A charitable man who would never turn away a beggar, he kept an alms pot in the house from which he would dispense money to those who came knocking. Her mother, a merchant's daughter from Venice, shared his concerns. The big family house set in a large garden of fruit trees was, as Mother Teresa described it, happy and unexceptional: a devout home devoted to the three children, of whom Agnes was the youngest. A serious child, she took no part in her brother's high spirits and mischievous adventures, although she was abidingly loyal to him and never told tales. This carefree family life came to an abrupt and tragic end when her father died unexpectedly, a victim of a suspected political assassination by poisoning. Her mother was grief-stricken and emotionally immobilized for several months, during which the assets in her father's business were stolen by his associate. Within a short period, the family had little more than the roof over their heads.

Gradually, Agnes's mother recovered and started a small business selling handwoven carpets and cloths. It was a pragmatic response to a dire situation. Much of this sensible resolve to get on with things even at the worst of times would later characterize her daughter's attitude. The family drew even closer to the church, finding there peace and succor while they mourned the loss of the man who had kept them secure. Agnes's mother took to spending a number of hours each day reciting the rosary, and would occasionally undertake the pilgrimage to a shrine for the Lady of Letnice on the outskirts of Skopje. Often her daughters joined her, the serious little Agnes an eager participant. Hours of prayer were not daunting to the young girl but a solace.

Agnes and her sister also joined various parish activities — the choir, the church library — and in her mid-teenage years, she became intrigued by the Sodality of the Blessed Virgin Mary, an organization for young people originally founded in the sixteenth century to spread Catholicism. Introduced into the parish by a new pastor, this branch of the Sodality had strong links to India.

For Agnes, the stories told of missionary work among the abject poor of that country had a particular resonance, especially when a group of Jesuits, recently returned from Bengal, recounted their time among the destitute and the poverty-stricken children of India. Agnes was moved both by their zeal and by the conditions of the people they sought to help. She joined a prayer group devoted to praying for the missionaries and their work in Bengal, but her curiosity went further. Tentative inquiries revealed that the way to India lay through the Loreto nuns. This international order had worked there since the nineteenth century, mainly in the field of education, but the chapter with jurisdiction over Bengal was Irish. Undaunted by these apparent complications, the teenage Agnes became increasingly convinced that her future waited among the poor of India, although she wasn't entirely sure that she wanted to become a nun.

At the age of eighteen she received a "calling," or what she thought was a calling. Doubting her own convictions, she prayed at the Letnice shrine and asked her pastor for guidance. He explained that the call of God was usually accompanied by a sense of deep joy. For Agnes, the bliss she was experiencing had to be the will of God. In later years she would tell biographers, "At eighteen I decided to leave home to become a nun. By then I realized my vocation was toward the poor. From then on, I have never had the least doubt of my decision. It was the will of God. He made the choice."[6]

Agnes duly applied to and was accepted into the Loreto Abbey at Rathfarnham in Dublin. A few months later, the small-town girl with no knowledge of English left Skopje by train. Her parting from her mother and sister was tearfully emotional. For despite the calling, her decision to leave her family, her town, the only world she knew, the place where she had been happy, was not made lightly. She would not see her distraught but proud mother again. As the figures on the platform receded, Agnes sat back and began a journey that had Calcutta as its objective.

After two months at Rathfarnham learning English, she sailed for Calcutta and onto the Loreto novitiate in the mountain resort of Darjeeling where she was to spend the next two years. Her days here passed quickly in prayer, in teaching and in learning not only English but Bengali and some Hindi. Toward the end of May 1931 she took her first vows of poverty, chastity, and obedience. She had previously changed her name to Teresa in Ireland when she became a postulant, and this name, like everything in her life, was far from an arbitrary whimsy. Inspired by St. Thérèse of Lisieux, renowned for her exceptional goodness in performing the humblest of tasks, Agnes had chosen the Spanish spelling as there was already a Sister Thérèse at Rathfarnham at the time. Her novitiate complete, Sister Teresa left Darjeeling for the Loreto convent at Entally, Calcutta. Six years later she took her final vows and taught quietly at the convent until the second calling came while she journeyed to the retreat at Darjeeling in 1946. The "real work" of Sister (later Mother) Teresa was soon to begin.

The start of Mother Teresa's new vocation among the poor was not easy. The indigent and the sick might be everywhere visible, but she had no organization to back her, no helpers, no building that could offer refuge to the people of the streets. Also she had very little money. She had left the convent with five rupees, but those had long since been spent on train fares and food. When she returned to Calcutta in December 1948 after her short medical internship at Patna, she had but a few rupees and sought shelter with the Little Sisters of the Poor. This gave her a place to sleep until she could find a room of her own.

In the meantime her pragmatism and commitment to small actions devoted to individuals brought her increasingly into contact with the people she wished to help. Without a room, let alone a blackboard or chalk, she began teaching children from the Motijhil slum under a tree. Using a stick she would draw the letters of the alphabet in the dirt and have the children recite the sounds. With each day her class grew, and each day passers-by would make small donations: a chair, a table, a blackboard, chalk. After a week, she received the comparatively large sum of a hundred rupees from a local priest and immediately used this to rent two rooms for her school. A few months later she opened a second school and was joined by the first of the nuns who would become known as the Missionaries of Charity.

As well as establishing the little schools, Mother Teresa was also tending to the sick, visiting people in hospitals and those lying ill at home. Tuberculosis (TB) and leprosy had cast a pall of disease over the slums, and wherever she looked she found sufferers. In a diary, she recorded meeting a woman in the streets who had been thrown out by her family because she was a leper. The woman's fingers had fallen off and she could no longer cook for herself. She spent her days begging and playing with a cat. "What a terrible sight," wrote a distressed Mother Teresa.[7] But that terrible sight strengthened her resolve. Whenever she came across people suffering from tetanus, cholera, meningitis, or TB, she would refer them to a hospital or call an ambulance. But there were many who did not need to be admitted to a hospital — they needed medicine or, for the terminally ill, a place to die with dignity.

To overcome the first problem she begged medicines from the city's pharmacists, and usually they obliged. Attending to the second instance was not as easily solved, but the need for a hospice impressed itself on her when she came upon the body of a man under a tree. She had noticed him earlier while passing in a tram and he had been alive, although sodden by the monsoon rains. An hour later he was dead. The pity welled up in Mother Teresa. How tragic to die alone. What if he had wanted to say something before he died? If only she had a place where people could die in dignity. These thoughts rushed through her mind as she stood beside the corpse, but she knew that to provide such refuges meant casting off the shame she felt at begging.

At first the need to beg had appalled her, but it was yet another humiliation that had to be absorbed and overcome if she was to continue her work. Not everybody was prepared to give; many abused her for acting irresponsibly and bringing the church into disrepute. But she persevered. Mendicancy was, after all, a long-established tradition in the culture, and Mother Teresa soon used it for her ends. She went on what she called begging expeditions to collect medicine, food, and clothing. She wrote begging letters to businesses, institutions, and the rich explaining her need for finance.

And yet behind this indefatigable appearance and dedication was a woman who occasionally doubted her abilities, but she was convinced that this was her mission and prayed regularly for guidance. At times she was tempted to look back to the comfort of the Loreto convent, especially when she heard people in the church questioning the value of her work among the poor. In the greater scheme of things, their arguments went, what worth to society were the poor? "Surely," Mother Teresa confided to her diary, "the poorest of the poor and the lowest of the low can have the love and devotion of us few. The Slum Sister they call me…"[8]

Indeed, she was weighing everything she did against the yardstick of those she sought to help. Yet even here the enormity of what she faced would claw at her heart. Not only was she teaching children, administering to the sick, and devoting hours to begging, but she was also searching for a place that would accommodate her envisioned Missionaries of Charity. That search meant trudging the streets. Sometimes this became almost too much to bear. "The poverty of the poor must be so hard for them," she wrote after a frustrating and tiring day. "When I went round looking for a home, I walked and walked till my legs and arms ached. I thought how they must also ache in body and soul looking for a home, food, help. Then the temptation grew strong. The palace buildings of Loreto came rushing into my mind. 'You have only to say a word and all that will be yours again,' the tempter kept on saying."[9] Even when she found accommodation and there was reason for optimism, the sheer aloneness of her efforts overwhelmed her. "Today, my God, what tortures of loneliness," she recorded in her diary. "I wonder how long my heart will suffer this. Tears rolled and rolled. Everyone sees my weakness. My God give me courage now to fight self and the tempter. Let me not draw back from the Sacrifice I have made of my free choice and conviction."[10]

Despite these private moments of anxiety, Mother Teresa had no intention of drawing back, especially not when each day brought with it the reality of Calcutta. And with the donation of the Creek Lane rooms by a generous catholic family of the parish, there was even more reason to persevere. Within a few months she was joined by her first postulates, both former pupils at St. Mary's, and her dream of the Missionaries of Charity began to flourish, although the congregation wasn't approved until 1950.

It wasn't easy. There might have been extra hands, but these were hard times. And although their vows — to which a new one was added that they were devoted to the "wholehearted and free service to the poorest of the poor" — and Mother Teresa's inspiration mentally and emotionally prepared the small group of sisters for self-denial, the demands were considerable.[11] They had to care for the sick and dying, they (and this included Mother Teresa) had to scrub the floors and the stairs daily, and there were times when food was scarce. Yet it was Mother Teresa's conviction that their times of want were God's providence, and invariably someone or some institution would come forward with food and clothing.

By February 1953, the Missionaries of Charity numbered twenty-seven sisters and moved from Creek Lane to a building in Lower Circular Road. That building became known as the "Motherhouse," and would become the center of an extraordinary religious order with outreach facilities in 130 countries.

At first the growth of the congregation was slow and restricted to Calcutta by canon law. After ten years, Mother Teresa was permitted to open her first house outside Calcutta, and by the end of 1960, there were twenty-five houses scattered across India. Four years later, with her society now responsible directly to the Vatican, she was invited to Venezuela by the Bishop of that country. The poverty she witnessed there moved her to open a center in Cocorote. It was the first step in a mission that would spread across the world.

In 1968 she opened her second overseas home in Rome, followed by two in Australia, then homes in London, Jordan, New York, Bangladesh, Northern Ireland, Gaza, Yemen, Ethiopia, Sicily, Papua New Guinea, the Philippines, Panama, Japan, and, in the 1990s, in South Africa and throughout Eastern

Europe, including her home country of Albania.

By the time of her death at the age of eighty-seven on September 5, 1997, the order which she had run for almost half a century was four thousand strong, not including an associated brotherhood of three hundred members and more than a hundred thousand volunteers. It cared for several thousand children and treated thousands of sick people each year. Mother Teresa's "life-long devotion to the care of the poor, the sick, and the disadvantaged [had become] one of the highest examples of service to our humanity," declared Nawaz Sharif, the Prime Minister of Pakistan, in an obituary.[12]

That service to humanity might have become of global proportions, but Mother Teresa never lost sight of individuals. Her concerns began with individuals in the streets of Calcutta and ended with a regard for individuals wherever they suffered hardships. When natural disasters struck anywhere in the world, she and her sisters would be among the first to respond with food, medicine, and clothing. She took little heed of personal risk, often entering disaster zones ahead of many aid organizations. Nor did wars deter her. When violence convulsed Pakistan in the early 1970s, she flew into the stricken country with two teams of sisters to set up clinics and shelters. When she heard of mentally handicapped children trapped without food and water at the height of the shelling in Beirut in 1982 in the most devastated part of the city, she went in a Red Cross van to rescue them. The snipers held their fire. She reacted similarly to the troubles in Belfast by personally opening shelters for those affected, and when the first Gulf War broke out in 1991, she addressed a letter to both U.S. President George Bush and Iraqi President Saddam Hussein begging them to stop the fighting. "I plead to you for those who will be left orphaned, widowed, and left alone because their parents, husbands, brothers, and children have been killed," she wrote. "I plead on bended knees for them. They will suffer, and when they do we will be the ones who are guilty for not having done all in our power to protect and love them."[13]

 Ironically, for someone who took no political sides, who eschewed power, who held no ambition for international status, she became, arguably, one of the most powerful women in the world. She had the ears of presidents and prime ministers, of kings, of the Pope, and of financiers and business executives of large multinational corporations. They would listen to her and invariably take heed.

She was, too, much honored, not only with honorary degrees, but with major awards — including a Nobel Peace Prize in 1979 and the U.S. Presidential Medal of Freedom in 1985 — that carried substantial financial benefits, all of which went immediately into her "real work." Such was her determination not to waste money that could better be used in the service of the poor that she even persuaded the Nobel Committee to forgo the customary awards banquet and donate the money to her organization. In like vein, many years previously, when Pope Paul VI had donated a limousine to her, she had promptly auctioned it. What good was a car when she could catch trams or walk? The money was directed to her Calcutta homes.

This attitude toward money characterized all her financial arrangements. Even in the latter years when money flowed in, funds never languished in bank accounts, nor was anything set aside for future adversities. Mother Teresa's policy was to spend money where it was needed immediately. "I don't want the work to become a business," she frequently remarked. "It must remain a work of love."[14] As for future adversities, she believed new donations would take care of those, and, unfailingly, they did.

But to understand the essential inspiration of Mother Teresa, nothing is truer of her regard for humanity than a comment she made to the TV anchor and journalist Malcolm Muggeridge in 1969: "I have come more and more to realize that it is being unwanted that is the worst disease that any human being can ever experience."[15] And it was in her efforts to comfort the unwanted that her abiding passion for humanity found its expression — an expression established in the founding years of her Missionaries of Charity that came to rest on three pillars: children, the ill, and the dying.

 Just as her initial attentions were to educating the children of the ghettos, so too she needed to care for those among them abandoned and unwanted. In the mid-1950s, she opened the first Shishu Bhavan, which would become a refuge for babies found dumped in trash cans, for children living in the sewers, and for those crippled or ill.

Soon police, hospitals, and social workers were bringing street children to the home. Mother Teresa welcomed them all. "For me, even if a child dies within minutes, that child must not be allowed to die alone and uncared for. Even an infant can feel human warmth."[16] In later years she would be equally vociferous in her condemnation of abortion, even if her attitude caused uneasiness among those who included abortion in their arguments for birth control. But for Mother Teresa, a life was a life, and all life was sacred and not to be violated.

Apart from the sheer exigencies of poverty, another of the main reasons for the abandonment of children in India was leprosy, and Mother Teresa's empathy went out to those regarded by society as unclean. But it was not until 1958 that she was able to establish a center for lepers.

In the Titagarh district of Calcutta, an informal shantytown of lepers had evolved, in many respects a human dumping ground. Often whole families ended up there, ostracized by their neighbors and communities. Many of these people needed medical treatment, but doctors were reluctant to treat them, and clinics and hospitals usually turned them away. The municipality handed the area over to Mother Teresa, who, with the pragmatism that kept her going in the most dire of circumstances, began the task of rehabilitating the slum and treating its inhabitants. It became known as the Gandhiji Prem Niwas, after the Mahatma whom Mother Teresa had never met but greatly admired.

Indeed, Mother Teresa and the Mahatma's attitudes toward humanity were determined by the same devotion to the poor and downtrodden, although for Mother Teresa it was also her love of God put into action. They both sought to identify with the poor by literally adopting their clothing: Mother Teresa, a simple handwoven sari, and Gandhi, a handspun dhoti. Like Gandhi she was unorthodox, courageous, and utterly dedicated. Like Gandhi she desired to give dignity to the humblest of lives. Nowhere was this more poignantly expressed than in her attitude toward the dying.

If in the early weeks of her "real work," the final moments of the dead man beneath the tree lingered in her thoughts, then the sight of a woman dying among the refuse, her body gnawed by rats and bitten raw by ants, aroused the deepest pity in Mother Teresa. She came across the woman as she returned to Creek Lane from a begging expedition and carried her to a local hospital. But the dying woman was refused admittance: the hospital had beds for the ill, not the dying.

Appalled by this experience, Mother Teresa asked the municipality for a building where she might tend to the dying. She was shown two halls attached to Calcutta's most famous Hindu temple erected to the goddess of death and destruction, Kali. Knowing that it was a site of worship and devotion to Hindus appealed to the nun who bridged all religious barriers. In 1952, long before the establishment of either the children's home or the leprosy center, she opened her shelter, the Kalighat Home for the Dying. Initially there was some hostility toward her from the Hindu community, but this soon stopped when Mother Teresa nursed a Kali priest dying of tuberculosis. Her intention was to allow people who "lived like animals" an opportunity "to die like angels," to die what she called "a beautiful death."[17]

In her Nobel acceptance speech she told a simple story meant to illustrate the work she and her sisters undertook, but which served equally, if unintentionally, to say much about the laureate: "One evening we went out and we picked up four people from the street. And one of them was in a most terrible condition. And I told the Sisters: 'You take care of the other three, I will take care of this one that looks worse.' So I did for her all that my love can do. I put her in bed, and there was such a beautiful smile on her face. She took hold of my hand, as she said one word only: 'Thank you' — and she died."[18] In this anecdote resides the humanity of the short wrinkled woman with the intense eyes and ready smile called Mother Teresa.

Mike Nicol
Cape Town, 2006

IT IS IN GIVING THAT WE RECEIVE.

We do not need guns and bombs to bring peace.
We need love and compassion.

{ Extract from address at Great St. Mary's, the University
Church, Cambridge, England, after receiving an
honorary degree, June

1977 }

Love begins at home, and it is not how much we do, but how much love we put into what we do.

We learn humility through accepting humiliations cheerfully.

The biggest disease today is not leprosy or tuberculosis, but rather the feeling of being unwanted, uncared for, and deserted by everybody. The greatest evil is the lack of love and charity, the terrible indifference toward one's neighbor...

A SMILE IS THE BEGINNING OF LOVE.

Do not allow yourself to be disheartened by any failure as long as you have done your best.

Joy is love — a joyful heart is the normal result of a heart burning with love, for she gives most who gives with joy.

Only humility will
lead us to unity,
and unity to peace.

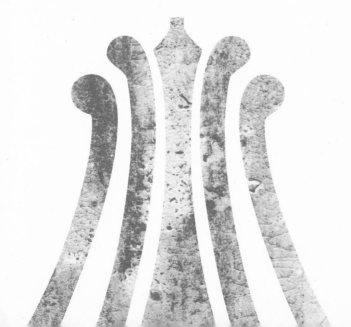

I do not agree with the big way of doing things. To us what matters is an individual. To get to love the person we must come in close contact with him. If we wait till we get the numbers, then we will be lost in the numbers. And we will never be able to show that love and respect for the person.

Be kind to each other — I prefer you make mistakes in kindness, than that you work miracles in unkindness.

{ Extract from a letter to the Sisters
1963}

JOY IS STRENGTH.

In these times of development, everybody is in a hurry and everybody's in a rush, and on the way there are people falling down, who are not able to compete. These are the ones we want to love and serve and take care of.

Nakedness is not only for a piece of cloth. Nakedness is for human dignity, for respect. Homelessness is not only for a home made of bricks. Homelessness is being rejected, unwanted, unloved, uncared for, having forgotten what is human love, what is human touch.

{ Extract from an address delivered in New York, May

1982}

Let us not make a mistake — that the hunger is only for a piece of bread. The hunger of today is so much greater: for love — to be wanted, to be loved, to be cared for, to be somebody.

We cannot condemn, judge, or speak
words that might hurt… By what right,
then, can we condemn anyone?

Let us be very sincere in our dealings with each other and have the courage to accept each other as we are.

Do the humble things with love and it will open the door for others!

If we really want to love others, we must first begin to love one another in our own home. Love begins at home, and so from here — from our own home — love will spread to my neighbor, in the street I live, in the town I live, in the whole world.

{ Extract from instructions to the Sisters

1988 }

HUMILITY IS TRUTH.

I beg you with my whole heart to work for, to labor for God's peace and to be reconciled with one another... In the short term there may be winners and losers in this war that we all dread, but that never can, nor never will justify the suffering, pain, and loss of life which your weapons will cause... please choose the way of peace... You may win the war but what will the cost be on people who are broken, disabled and lost.

{ Letter to Presidents George H. W. Bush and Saddam Hussein, January

1991}

Love is a fruit always in season, and no limit is set. Everyone can reach this love.

What you can do, we cannot do, and what we can do, you cannot do, but together we can do something beautiful.

How do we love? Not in big things, but in small things with great love.

{ Extract from instructions to the Sisters }
1984}

PEACE BEGINS WITH A SMILE

All our words will be useless

 unless they come from within.

If all the money that is being spent on finding ways to kill people was used instead to feed them and house them, clothe them and educate them — how beautiful that would be. We are too often afraid of the sacrifices we might have to make. But where there is true love, there is joy and peace.

{ Extract from a press release to the Cairo Conference,

1994 }

I repeat that it is not what we do, but how much love we put into doing it.

{ Extract from an address delivered in Rome, May

1982}

TO WORK WITHOUT LOVE IS SLAVERY.

We can do no great things —

only small things with great love.

Never let anyone come to you without coming away better and happier.

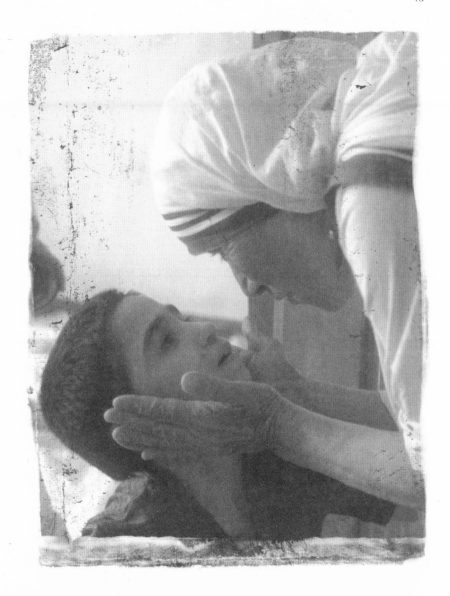

Everybody should see kindness in your face, in your eyes, in your smile, in your warm greeting.

INTENSE LOVE DOES NOT MEASURE — IT JUST GIVES.

We cannot solve all the problems in the world, but let us never bring in the worst problem of all, and that is to destroy love.

We must never be preoccupied with the future. There is no reason to be so.

Thoughtfulness is the beginning of great sanctity.

We know that if we really want to love
we must learn to forgive.

We must never think any one of us is indispensable.

We have no time to listen to the poor — often they have to come again and again — walk long distances — sick, tired, in pain — to tell us of their want — of their suffering, and we, because we are busy about many things, we have no time to sit at their feet and listen… To all those who suffer and are lonely — give them always a happy smile — give them not only your ears but also your heart.

Kindness has converted more people than zeal, science, or eloquence.

Love the poor. Do you know the poor of your place, of your city? Find them. Maybe they are right in your own family.

Hunger is not only for a piece of bread.
Hunger is for love.

WORKS OF LOVE ARE ALWAYS WORKS OF PEACE.

We are all capable of good and evil.
We are not born bad: everybody has
something good inside. Some hide it,
some neglect it, but it is there.

CHARITY

A royalty from the sale of this book will be donated to the Tygerberg Children's Hospital and Philani Clinic on behalf of Archbishop Desmond Tutu.

ACKNOWLEDGMENTS

The publisher is grateful for permissions to reproduce material subject to copyright. Every effort has been made to trace the copyright holders and the publisher apologizes for any unintentional omission. We would be pleased to hear from any not acknowledged here and undertake to make all reasonable efforts to include the appropriate acknowledgment in any subsequent editions.

All writings of Mother Teresa of Calcutta © The Mother Teresa Center, exclusive licensee throughout the world of the Missionaries of Charity for the works of Mother Teresa. Used with permission. Images used with permission of following copyright holders: pp. 6, 9, 12, 19, 20, 56 and 82 © Getty Images; p. 15 © Time Life Pictures/Getty Images; p. 37 © AFP/Getty Images; p. 30 © Kapoor Baldev/Sygma/CORBIS; pp. 42–43 and 63 © JP Laffont/Sygma/CORBIS; pp. 48, 69 and cover © Bettmann/CORBIS; p. 75 © CORBIS. Image of Desmond Tutu (p. 2) © Matt Hoyle.

The publisher would like to thank the following people and organizations.

Archbishop Tutu for his generous support of the Ubuntu Collection; and Lynn Franklin, Archbishop Tutu's literary agent, for her kind assistance with the series.

The Mother Teresa Center, for their kind help in authenticating the quotations in this book. The Mother Teresa of Calcutta Center is a non-profit organization established and directed by the religious family founded by Blessed Teresa of Calcutta, the Missionaries of Charity. The Center's aim is to stand as a centralized and authoritative source of information on Mother Teresa, to facilitate the spread of authentic devotion to her, and to safeguard her words and image from misuse and abuse.

Mike Nicol for his insightful biographical essay. Mike Nicol has had a distinguished career both in South Africa and in the UK as an author, journalist and poet. He is the author of four critically acclaimed novels published in South Africa, the U.S., the UK, France and Germany. His best-known nonfiction work is his book on *Drum* magazine, *A Good-Looking Corpse* (Secker & Warburg, 1991), widely regarded as one of the most compelling accounts of the vibrant culture in the black townships of the 1950s.

Thanks also to Jenny Clements for text research and Simon Elder for picture research.

SELECT BIBLIOGRAPHY

Chawla, Navin, *Mother Teresa* (Sinclair-Stevenson, London, 1992).
Gorree, Georges & Barbier, Jean, *For the Love of God — Mother Teresa of Calcutta* (Veritas Publications, Dublin, 1974).
— *The Love of Christ — Spiritual Counsels* (HarperCollins, New York, 1982).
— *Love Without Boundaries — Mother Teresa of Calcutta* (Our Sunday Visitor, Huntingdon, IN, 1974).
Muggeridge, Malcolm, *Something Beautiful for God* (Collins, London, 1971).
Rai, Raghu & Chawla, Navin, *Mother Teresa — The Life and Work of Mother Teresa* (Element Books, Shaftsbury, 1996).
Spink, Kathryn, *For the Brotherhood of Man Under the Fatherhood of God* (Colour Library International, New Malden, United Kingdom, 1981).
— *In the Silence of the Heart — Meditations by Mother Teresa* (SPCK, London, 1983).
Archives — Mother Teresa Center.

NOTES FOR THE BIBLIOGRAPHIC ESSAY

1 Chawla, Navin, *Mother Teresa*, 19; 2 Muggeridge, Malcolm, *Something Beautiful for God*, 85; 3 Chawla, Navin, *Mother Teresa*, 19; 4 Muggeridge, Malcolm, *Something Beautiful for God*, 118; 5 Spink, Kathryn, *For the Brotherhood of Man Under the Fatherhood of God*, 22; 6 Rai, Raghu and Chawla, Navin, *Mother Teresa — The Life and Work of Mother Teresa*, 24; 7 Chawla, Navin, *Mother Teresa*, 40; 8 Ibid. 44; 9 Ibid. 47; 10 Ibid. 48; 11 Ibid. 60; 12 Foundation of the Missionaries of Charity, http://en.wikipedia.org/wiki/Mother_Teresa; 13 Chawla, Navin, *Mother Teresa*, 218; 14 Ibid. 74; 15 Muggeridge, Malcolm, *Something Beautiful for God*, 99; 16 Chawla, Navin, *Mother Teresa*, 118; 17 Spink, Kathryn, *For the Brotherhood of Man Under the Fatherhood of God*, 43; 18 Ibid. 233.